Love Her Right

Poetry & Prose

By Daniel Mercury

Connect with Daniel Mercury

Email: writesmercury@gmail.com

Facebook: www.facebook.com/DanielMercuryWrites/

Instagram: www.instagram.com/mercury_writes/

Cover Design by Gözdem Perrichet

ISBN: 9781977018243

Love Her Right is a compilation of poems and prose by Daniel Mercury. In his debut release, the author's whole and undivided attention is on women "that men have no choice but to love beyond reason, for they blow their minds away with their scent, taste, sheer presence..."

Daniel Mercury's words are tender, passionate, thought-provoking... and addictive, inviting readers to dive into the sensual journey that *Love Her Right* is.

Foreword

Daniel Mercury is a romantic at heart with a twist, dark and enchanting.

His sensual poetry is both decadent and powerful while his words show no mercy as they delve into the inner workings of the female psyche speaking directly to the hopeless romantic in you and the passions that lurk within your heart, mind, body and soul.

Daniel Mercury weaves his dramatic and oh-so magical flair into his poetry leaving you a little breathless, a little starstruck, always wanting more of him.

N.R. Hart, Author of *Poetry and Pearls*

Table of Contents

Part I Mind

To seduce a woman

you need to hijack her imagination

and then leave her breathless

with an ache to fill in the blanks…

Indifference

And eventually she will stop
giving you one chance
after another,
for every time the disappointment
cuts deeper,
breaks her heart a little more
and the fractures you've created in it
are about to reach
a dangerous point of indifference
where you turn into someone
she used to know, but no more.

Bright & Hot

Passion ran bright and hot
through this one:
she gave everything she was,
be that in love or every other part of her life.
She often needed a reminder
to keep some of that fire
burning for herself.

I like her odds

Behind those eyes
are secrets
she will never share
with ease and a smile.
Underneath this skin
lives a heart
she will never trust again
to unsteady hands.
But it beats ever-so strongly
against every adversity,
and I like her odds.

Need no words

It's not about speaking

the same language,

it's about sharing

thoughts and feelings

that need no words…

Commitment is not a game

You have to understand now
that if we ever find ourselves
at a crossroads of our togetherness,
I will not let you go or walk away myself
without one hell of a fight.
We will retract our steps
and correct wherever we have erred.
I might have been a player once,
but you are the one who have taught me
that commitment is not a game.

You are not a match

How many times more

will you burn out

before realizing

that you are not a match

people can strike

whenever they feel cold?

Be vulnerable with me

Be vulnerable with me;
talk to me about your nightmares
in the harshness of daytime.
Don't hide your chaos,
introduce your mad thoughts to me–
one by one.
I will not judge you,
for I too have my own demons,
carry my own burdens.

Playing dirty

Those hands of mine
were made to play dirty
and hold her gently,
and it's a good thing
she doesn't mind that sometimes
it seems one and the same.

Hearts empty and bodies cold

Another smoke-filled night
with pulsating needs
that find no rhythm within your veins.
What do they want that you don't?
What do you want that they can't reach?
Connection. Love. Meaning.
Trust that this life is more than a moment
spent on chasing fleeting pleasures
that leave hearts empty and bodies cold.

A privilege

I wonder what it is
that people try to avoid
by not attaching themselves
to another human being.
Loneliness is not such a treat
that I would not cede my right to it
instantly.
And if love doesn't work,
heartbreak is a bullet I will take
and wear like a badge
for the privilege of feeling deeply.

The force of nature

She would dance in the rain
and laugh every time
a thunder struck
until I cared not for the storm,
for she was the force of nature
I couldn't take my eyes off.

Strength

Strength is rarely inborn.
There is usually a high price
to be paid for it,
and walking through the depths of hell
is not optional.
You can't expect people
to be strong
and still come to you
with innocence in their eyes.

When you love a writer

When you love a writer
you need to read between their words
all that they leave unsaid.
You have to learn
to collect drops of ink
from the pages filled,
for that's where their hearts
beat the strongest.

No shame in her ashes

You thought her an easy mark,
for she knew the pain of a heartbreak.
What you didn't know
is that a strong, deeply feeling woman
like her
gets burned only once,
and there is not an ounce of shame
in the trail of ashes
she leaves behind.

No holds barred

Poets will love you
with no holds barred,
for we don't fear a heartbreak.
On the best days
we will write with affection,
on the worst–the ink will flow red
from the core of our wounded hearts.

I hate your tears

When I say I hate your tears,
it doesn't mean I never want to see them again.
What I should be telling you
is that every drop is a punch to my ego
for my inability to stem the flow.
But when I say I hate when you use *okays*
as band aids to patch up your wounds
in order to placate me–
I really mean it.
I will take tears over a fake smile
any day of the week.

Poetry and her

She wraps poetry
around her body,
smearing tender words
on her skin
in a desperate attempt
to feel loved.

I've been wondering...

I've been wondering about you a lot:
I want to know
what makes you drop your guard
and when you feel the most alive.
I crave to know the secrets
flickering behind your eyelids–
those you believe well hidden
behind the curtain of your lashes.
Most of all, I burn to hear
that it is me you think about
when the lights go off at night
and you stroke yourself to sleep…

A mermaid

She dreamed
about becoming a mermaid,
for she would no longer have to
justify and explain the depths
she liked to swim in
to shallow minds.

Melody of her

Her melody was a mere humming to you,
nothing but a background noise.
Fool,
a goddamn fool.
You were never man enough
to comprehend the song
locked in her throat and grasp
the meaning behind her lyrics.
You need to know
how to coax a woman like her to sing.
What you carelessly rejected as a chore
is my privilege now.

Clean slate

You are not an empty canvas
for the wickedest of my desires.
Not a white wall
to pin my hopes and dreams on.
But I got lost in your calm blue sea
to the point where my storm
rages no more.
It's a chance to wipe my slate clean–
something I can't walk away from.

Either the one or no one

I can't feast on your *maybe*

and drink down your *someday*.

I'm no longer a *someone,* or an *anyone,*

a scratch to your itch.

I'm either *the one,*

or don't ever call me again.

Ink-streaked fingers

She lives somewhere
between an epic love story
and the barren state
of feeling loveless,
walking pages of romance novels
and wishful thinking
on her ink-streaked fingers.

I'm fine

She wants to tell you
that she feels broken,
but she knows
you would try to patch up her fractures
and that would have felt
like a slap in the face
telling her she is not good enough
the way she is.
She wants to cry,
but is too afraid that once
this river of sadness started flowing
there would be no dam to stop it.
She wants so much and so damn little,
but in the end *I'm fine*
is all she ever says.

A good look in the mirror

She kept waiting for someone
who would make sense
out of her mess,
someone to unearth
the levels of her inner light,
forgetting that all she needed
was to take a good look at herself
in the mirror.

Come on, test me...

You are not difficult to love, darling,
you just need to understand that not any lover will do.
Some are good only for a smooth sailing,
they will try to impress you by reciting words
written by long dead poets–
and there is nothing wrong with that,
but you are not that kind of a girl.
You need a rebel, a pirate
who will write a book of his own
with every dirty trick in it
he is going to use to get you.
A fighter to ride out
the unpredictability of a storm ahead,
which you will call forth just to test him.
Come on, test me.

Her smile

I love watching her smile grow wider
until it blooms into a laugh–
so deep and so true,
I want to give her more reasons
to keep it going,
and last just a moment longer…

Facing yourself

There are days
when she is ready to take
on the world and conquer it
with a breathtaking confidence.
There are also mornings
she can hardly leave the safety of her bed
and face her own reflection in the mirror.
I love her–always,
but admire her the most
on those mornings,
for nothing is as scary and hard
as facing yourself.

Witching hour

You, my dear,

need the kind of love

that will bring you

past the witching hour

when your wayward mind

likes to play tricks on you

the most,

whispering its seductive untruths

right into your ear…

Childlike ability

I admire her almost childlike ability
to find joy
in the most insubstantial of things,
and the way her mind can dive
into the complexity of any thought,
still feeling at home
where so many would have struggled for air.

No other way

Shallow is not a word
she is intimately acquainted with,
for she loves, thinks and lives
passionately
with a depth
that often makes her hurt.
Yet, she still wouldn't have it
any other way.

Beauty and the Beast

Love and *forever*

might be what you wish for,

but they are also words

that people will use against you

to get what they want,

and then leave you to bite the dust,

wondering what just happened

for the rest of your life.

Wake up, darling,

for no matter your beauty,

sometimes a beast is just a beast.

Past bearing

Never think that those
who feel and live deeply
need their space
because they love you less.
The truth is they love you more–
more than it's safe, more than it's wise–
and sometimes the touch of your skin
feels abrasive against their own
because emotions contained underneath it
are heightened past bearing.

Behind the closed doors

I will be the strength
standing in front of you
to shield your vulnerability
from the harshness of this world,
but I want to be your weakness
behind the closed doors.

Never defeated

She loses herself
in the chaos of her thoughts,
slaying monsters I know nothing of
and battling her way through
the corridors of everyday madness.
I've seen her bruised and bloodied,
but never defeated.

I will wait for you

And I will wait for you,
not because I am patient–
God knows I am anything but that.
Not because we have forever,
for all we have are mere moments
that will never be enough.
No, I will wait for you,
because you are worth it all
and we will live our eternity
in the time meant for us.

The strength of a tsunami

Some want to believe
that soft means weak
and I feel sorry for those fools.
I touch and appreciate her softness,
and never let myself forget
that the spine of steel
covered by the silky flesh
is anything but pliable.
She might be smooth as water,
but she has the strength of a tsunami.

Never-ending chatter

She goes silent at times,

but don't let it fool you

into believing she has nothing to say,

for those are the instances

her mind is the loudest,

and she is busy listening

to the never-ending chatter of her thoughts.

Socially challenged

She likes to walk

the borders of solitude

and skim her hand

through the surface of crowds

in search of one person

who would feel as socially challenged

as she does at times.

I will raise a glass to her

It's not that her softness
translates into weakness.
It's not that she doesn't know
how to get her hands dirty,
or can't get brutal.
It's just that bringing her
to the edge of her tolerance
takes longer,
but once there–
she will not back down,
she will savage you.
And I will just sit this one out,
stay on the sidelines
and raise a glass to her.

You are a rock

Whatever you are told, remember–
you are a rock–
when they treat you with tenderness,
they can flow around you
softly like water.
Only those
with intentions to break you
will cut themselves
over your sharp edges.

Temporary people

She stumbled,

she fell,

she came apart,

healed her broken bones

and gathered her shattered dreams.

And she learned,

My God, did she ever,

but it was the kind of a lesson that

put an ache in her

for the eternity to come,

and made her wary

of temporary people

that are not worth the pain.

She falls silent at times

She falls silent at times–
don't force her to speak.
Know that she tries to hold off
the scream from within
for a bit longer.
Pushing her in those moments
will only widen the space
between her need to be understood,
and your inability to do so.

A wrong pair of eyes

Perhaps
when you find yourself
not liking your own reflection
anymore,
it means you've chosen
a wrong pair of eyes
to use as a mirror.

Oh-so tired

She is strong,

she is capable,

but oh-so tired of proving it

and carrying the weight of the world

on her shoulders

just because she can.

Maybe-love

"Don't bring the debris

of your maybe-love

to my door ever again,"

she told him.

"I will not let you in,

for your presence lasts

but a moment

and the damage it makes

takes too long to repair and overcome."

Someone else's shadow

You better leave her alone

in the twilight,

for she is not afraid of the dark

as much as being nothing

but someone else's shadow.

The sky of her

She wants a man

who will look at the sky of her

and recognize the clouds

brewing on the horizon

where everyone else sees

only brightness of the sun.

A lost boy

She'd spent decades
on learning herself
until she's finally understood
who she is
and found the skin she's in
comfortable enough.
Trust me when I tell you this:
she is not going to change for you now,
just because you are a lost boy
who doesn't know
what the fuck he wants,
much less what to do
with a woman like her.
Step down and don't waste her time.

She won't stop

She might not have

all the answers

today or even tomorrow,

but she will not stop

asking questions

until she has it all figured out.

Don't call it *love*

You might not be so fond of those nights
filled with nothing
but a raging storm of chaos in her mind;
she is scared of the ferocity of it herself at times.
But you can't choose to be around
only when reason comes back to rule her life,
and call it *love*.

Poetry & happily ever after

She lives for poetry,

romance and happily ever after

in a world

that tries its damnedest

to disregard their existence.

And you wonder why...

And you wonder why she's so quiet these days...
She's shared her thoughts with you,
declared her feelings,
and you took them,
you took it all,
sharpened them into a knife,
loaded a gun with them
and turned the weapon against her.
And you wonder why she's so quiet these days...

Can't find words

When her tears soak through my shirt
and her sadness burns my skin,
I mix the hues of it
with the ink in my pen,
trying to put together
what she feels,
but can't find words for.

Becoming is not pretty

Let's be honest:
becoming is never pretty.
It's a hard work that leaves no one unscathed
and with hands clean.
It' pain in the middle of the night
that stays until the next morning
and it's the kind of an ache
that echoes even longer than that.
It's blood on your hands, on your knees
after clawing your way through the process
and crawling to your destination point.
But the pain, the blood, it's all worth it.
The strength is yours
and nobody can ever deny you that.

True to herself

She gets quiet sometimes
in a way that speaks volumes
without uttering the actual words.
Those are times she is trying
to tame the wildness of her thoughts,
calm the storm of her emotions,
and through it all, remain true to herself.

Heaven & hell

Ah look:
she can eat, drink and breathe without you
just fine,
even though your parting words
suggested otherwise.
She can laugh and dance again,
even though you wished she stayed as miserable
as you made her feel all this time.
She finally knows love,
and swears it feels like heaven,
even though you told her to go to hell.
Ah look:
that's where you are now,
and it's the best place
for an asshole like you.

Pretty has never done if for me

Your soul might be dirty
and heavy with sins,
but it's passionate, it's honest,
it's yours.
Pretty has never done it for me
and it's not going to start now.
They can keep their pristine lies,
I want you
with your throat burning
from the rawness of your truth.

Sin on our skin

I don't care where you'd been;
we've all been to hell and back,
still trying to wash off the soot
and sin from our skin.
The only thing I am interested in
is where you are heading from here
and is there room enough for two.

A life lived

I like the scent of survival
on your skin,
it smells like places seen
and a life truly lived.
It feels like understanding
and home.

Comfortable in silence

She might enjoy
talking for hours
about everything and nothing,
but she will settle down only
with someone
who makes her equally comfortable
in silence.

One hell of a job

A strong woman
will not be satisfied
with a few fancy words
carelessly thrown around
like crumbs for starved and desperate.
She needs nightmares along the dreams,
lost temper with the belly of every matter.
She needs raw and real
because raw and real is what she is,
and while she might appreciate
your need to protect her,
she doesn't really need it,
she's been doing one hell of a job of it herself.

A survivor

Someone has stolen
the smile from her lips,
snuffed out
the sparkle in her eyes,
picked up a few feathers
from her wings.
But she still stands proud
on her two feet
and I never treat her as a fragile,
breakable thing,
for a survivor deserves respect,
never pity.

Eternal night

If you harm a woman's confidence
with your carelessness,
her light will slowly dim
like the sun
that hangs a little lower
every day
until one morning
it is an eternal night
you wake up to.

Without judgment

It's easier to write

about what hurts

than to talk about it,

for I can stare at a blank page

at my leisure

and it stares back at me

without judgment

Part II Soul

Baby, leave your clothes on.

It is your soul that I want to strip bare tonight…

Past indiscretions

I forget my soul's past indiscretions
when it senses the closeness of yours.
I forget aches and echoes of trouble
that I might or might not have been a part of.
Your presence pours sweet oblivion
over everything I've known
and seduces me with the promise
of better yet to come.

Night & day

She is a late night–
wide awake and alone,
over thinking in the place of emotions
too big and too scary to embrace.
She is a day–
sleep deprived and surrounded by people,
pretending to have it all under control
and hiding the white-knuckled grip
on everything that keeps slipping away.

A lone wolf

I would have been okay on my own–
the whole lone wolf thing
had always worked just fine for me–
but then you've brought the kind of order to my chaos
that doesn't negate it,
doesn't try to fix it,
and that acceptance makes me a better man.

Eyes wide-shut

She was a wild girl with big eyes wide open,
always ready to propel herself
into another adventure.
They could neither contain,
nor comprehend her gypsy soul,
for their eyes were wide-shut.

Not afraid of your depths

I will not ask you to smile
when all I can see is sadness
swimming in the pools of your eyes.
I would rather hold my breath and dive in.
I don't care if you let me float on the surface
or decide to pull me down
with another wave of melancholy yet to hit.
Shallow waters are for little girls and boys
and I am not afraid of your depths.

The edge of uncertainty

If his touch is not enough

to bring you back

from the edge of uncertainty,

he is not the one

that should be touching you…

The endless night

Don't let the stars in her eyes fool you,

for she carries the endless night in her soul as well,

fighting her own battles in silence.

Especially when all she wants

is to scream her pain out loud.

Bohemian souls

Being a free-spirited woman
in a world that cares not for bohemian souls,
is a precarious thing.
Being a man of such a woman is even harder:
it's a mad dance on a tightrope,
a constant search for equilibrium
between protecting what's yours,
while making sure she has enough space and freedom
to remain true to herself.

Stay with me

It's getting dark.
Stay with me and let us not talk
about what hurts,
but allow the quiet night around us
soothe the pain
the way that words never will.

Fluent in tears

She was fluent in tears;

the eloquent drops

have always told stories

of those aching places

where words

would fear to venture.

Phantom fingers

Baby,

I will never exorcise my ghosts,

for you are one of them

and I have a fondness

for your phantom fingers

still stroking my soul.

Your generosity

You burn so brightly at times–
your flames are nearly licking at the sky now–
and I wonder the price you have to pay
for being a candle in the darkness of this world.
I put my mouth to yours,
deepen the kiss
until my tongue touches yours.
Ash is all I taste
under the layers of your generosity.

Nothing compliant about her

Let me tell you something
about the perfect woman you want:
she will not sit modestly, looking pretty
and waiting for you to be the prince to her princess.
She has her own battles to fight
and her own dragons to slay
before she decides to settle down with you.
And even then she won't surrender to your very will,
for there is nothing compliant about her.

The moon & the wolf

Baby,

I have never been the wolf.

You made me the moon

when you ran to me

howling my name.

Ready to heal

Through my dreams she walks,
dripping salt from the wounds
this world has inflicted
upon her sensitive soul.
She is ready to heal.

At full tilt

One day,

we will run into each other

at full tilt.

That's when you will come

to understand

that forces of nature

cannot be stopped…

The eye of the storm

I am the storm
that will rain with a vengeance,
striking lightning right and left
when my temper slips out of its leash.
Soaked through, she stands unflinching,
for she is the eye of my hurricane,
and while the whole world goes to hell
it is calm and well within this private torment
caused by our own brand of madness.

Head held high

And while some people
would have let my sins
be a ball and chain of shame at their ankles,
she had them made into a necklace
that she insists on wearing with pride
and head held high.

The mystery of ink

In the black mystery of ink
she hides her deepest desires,
waiting for a man
capable of reading
between the lines…

Her artistic soul

Her artistic soul is always messy,
but there is order to her chaos
that will turn your world upside down,
and you are going to thank her for it.
You will find wild and unfinished thoughts
in her tangled hair,
wake up to her arguing with the moon
in the middle of the night,
but you will never resent her for any of it,
for her loving life to the fullest is catching
and believe me–you never want to be cured.

Love her, teach her...

See her

at those times she loses the sight of herself.

Hear her

when she stops hearing her own voice.

Love her

when she can't connect with any part of her being

that knows the emotion.

Teach her...

She calls me back

She calls me back
when I wander off too far.
She pulls me back
when my roaming ways
take the best of me.
She anchors me with her love,
but never turns her feelings and care
into the steel bars of imprisonment.

Her inner turmoil

She wears calmness
in the middle of the storm
and it fits her perfectly,
just like chaos seems to be
the natural color of her eyes
when everything subsides and falls in line,
except her inner turmoil.

Longing & regret

She loved herself
where no one else dared to:
in the eye of the storm,
in the middle of every moonless night,
in every corner filled with shadows.
And the light she has found
in the most unlikely places was such
that it filled all those who had failed to love her
with longing and regret.

All that lies underneath

She thought herself to be a patchwork
of her favorite songs
with heartbreakingly sad lyrics.
But what she really is made of,
is the melody
she has been humming all along
about mended hearts and bones
and all the strength
that lies underneath.

A staccato rhythm

Her heart beats a staccato rhythm
of fear in her throat,
it does it quite often,
but she is still unstoppable
and keeps moving forward,
even if it is one small step at a time.

She dreams...

She dreams of love
that would decorate
every heartbreak
she has ever gone through
with understanding
instead of deepening
the scars already there.

A lifetime

All she has ever wanted

was a lover

who would not only take her passion,

but offer his fire in return

that could last a lifetime.

You can't fathom

Maybe what you took
for her desire to burn
was nothing more and nothing less
than her need to be reduced to ashes,
so she could rise from all her yesterdays
and come back with the kind of strength
that you can't fathom tomorrow.

Aching places

I focus on the language of your eyes
at those times
I can't understand your words.
Whenever they overflow
with salty droplets,
I try to translate my way through them
to the aching places in your soul.

Two strangers

I don't know who you are
or where you are,
but perhaps in this very moment,
our hearts beat in a rhythm
that sounds similar enough,
and our thought patterns match.
Isn't it something?
Two strangers–
somewhere that could be anywhere.
I don't know about you,
but it just made me feel less alone.

Fast love

In a world focused on fast love
and instant gratification,
there are still those souls
that choose the path of romance
and take their sweet time
while they are on it.

Your soul still speaks to me

Your wings
might have caught on some soot
from those times you got burned,
but your soul still speaks to me
about wonders and the good in people
that you always try to see
regardless their attempts to prove you wrong.

Listen to her

Listen to her:

that's the least you can do

to prove that you are there

for more than only good times.

She might still love fairy tales,

but she doesn't expect anyone

to solve her problems for her,

just being there when she figures herself out.

She knows no defeat

Her bones are fragile,

but strong.

Ordinary, yet magnificent.

That's what makes her fall so hard

and rise with a fury

that knows no defeat…

Dream catcher

She is a dreamer at heart–

spinning beautiful reveries

asleep and awake alike.

And the one thing

every beautiful romantic truly needs,

is a dream catcher…

An old soul in a modern world

Hers is an old soul in a modern world:
she wants romance and candle light.
I let the molten wax drip onto her naked skin,
and in the dark is where we write
our own version of love story…

I promise you

The place of your breaking
is not going to be your defining point.
It's not the end of your way,
not the bedrock of your identity.
It's simply a part of you,
like those freckles and that smile of yours–
neither more nor less important.
You might have stumbled for a moment there,
but I promise you
that your feet will carry you on.

Sands of her dreams

She seems always in conflict
with herself:
her gypsy soul craves adventure
while her love-starved heart
dreams of roots.
She is trying to build a house
on the sands of her dreams
that keep drifting away…

Judgmental world

You might think that you have her
all figured out because she allowed you
a glimpse of her soul
and let you take a peek at her heart.
But that's just a sliver of a person that she is.
She has many nooks and cranes to hide in
when the world gets too judgmental
and harsh about little does it know…

Bold strokes

I love how our naked bodies
danced together
with no witness save the moon
and its wicked light.
But absolutely nothing can compare
to the feeling of your fingertips
hesitantly touching my soul,
lingering and then getting more bold
with every stroke...

Not mastered yet

One of these days
you will understand your call,
for your path is written
in your bones and soul
in a language
you simply haven't mastered yet.

Ebbs & Flows

She is drawn to water;

to its ebbs and flows,

how it never stops to change,

always becoming,

with nothing but a promise in its waves.

She is drawn to water

because she is just like that herself.

Sunrise & Sunset

She is not the sunrise kind of a girl,

neither is she the sunset.

Maybe she is both,

but you will never learn,

for you tried to label and limit her.

This is how you lose your chance.

Seemingly an ugly cocoon

Mistakes–
those flawed shards of glass–
cut her deeply more times
than she cares to recall,
but they've also created
the most stunning mosaic
of who she is today,
a beautiful butterfly that has emerged
from seemingly an ugly cocoon.

A slip of a girl

She might have looked
like a slip of a girl,
but deep down she was a fire-breather
with mighty flames burning in her bones
pushing her to not only accept challenges,
life kept throwing at her,
but to dare it right back.

Careful now...

Careful now darling,

dark has ways

of creeping in undetected

until it's too late

and it's everywhere,

and it's heavy to carry around,

and leaves us no choice

but to bear it in silence,

with a fucking bright smile on our numb lips.

You are magic

You are magic, my dear,
and the worst harm
this world can inflict upon you
is to start snuffing out the stars within you
until all the light fades away
and you start to believe
you are but ordinary…

Against all odds

She is an angel, I think,

maybe a butterfly.

Ah no, she is a moth–

drawn to everything that spells danger

and whispers her name.

I can see those wings

beating against all odds,

smoldering,

but the flames do her no harm.

She is rising again.

Your brand of insanity

Some will say
your intensity is overwhelming,
the chaos of your thoughts,
the madness in your blood–
frightening.
Others are out there looking
just for your brand of insanity
and would give anything to be lost in it.

She will burn the book

She will burn the book

you've written for her

to its very last page.

She will burn it down

and write her own,

for she is tired of being told

how her story is supposed to unravel.

The next best thing

She has a gypsy soul;
always more than ready
to run after the next best thing.
She inhales air, exhales wildness.
It's her heart that is off-beat,
dressed in melancholy,
keeping to desolated roads.

Madman & beast

I'm not a madman, I'm not a beast.
Maybe I am both.
The craving to taste your soul
keeps teasing me into insanity,
seducing into forgetting my humanity
I want to shed like too tame skin
that can't house this need any longer.

A falling star of her

She doesn't know the day or time,

for it matters not

since her soul is encased in a forever kind of night.

It's the intensity of those eyes

that invites you to take a dive into the dark,

the unknown, the unforgiving

where it all burns, ruptures and cascades.

A falling star of her.

You have light

You have light
even if it feels a shade or two
darker than it should at times,
even when it flickers
and threatens to go off.
You have light.

I like broken people

I've always been attracted to things
that most would not give a second thought to,
for appearance is all
that too many care about these days–
as if chasing perfect would make them
shine better for the effort it takes.
I like broken people, but I understand those
who try to avoid them
because you either connect with pain or you don't.
I like uneven, jagged edges of the gulfs
that keep sharpening their teeth
no matter how far away from the brink you stand.
I like the monstrous faces of our fears
that appear always bigger
with no rear-view mirror in sight.

I like it all, as a reminder of everything
we’ve come through
and that there is no rest for the wicked.
Talk to me about your pain,
for I too, carry scars
that has marked me forever.

Shallow doesn't cut it

She is an old soul,

you can't expect her to fill the space–

vacated by romance and loyalty–

with meaningless sex and shallow connection

that won't last until morning.

The imprint of your soul

Any lover
can run his fingers
through your hair,
stroke them over your skin.
But how many
carry the imprint of your soul
on their fingertips?

Break the bars

She reinvents herself constantly,

not because she is flighty

or can't make up her mind,

but because life is often too confining

for those souls

who wish to live fully

and break the bars of their cages.

She is meant to stand out

They admired her chaos for its honesty,

but tried to add some polish to it,

so she could blend in,

because too much honesty is too hard to take

by those who are used to lies and live in denial.

Fools,

she is meant to stand out

until their eyes tear up.

Wrong spell

I see so much magic in you,
don’t let the non-believers
convince you
there is no such thing,
just because they don’t know
the right spell.

A wild one

She might be down to earth
and rooted in reality
by her responsibilities,
but her soul is a wild one;
always set on finding magic
in sunsets and sunrises
that others take for granted.

She blossoms

She blossoms
even though her bones are cracking
and her heart has been broken.
She blossoms,
for her spirit is honed by every fracture.

At bay

Don't tell her that you love her
when she looks her best,
for she will think it's perfection
that you are after
and will always try to keep
the true beauty of her vulnerability
at bay.

Old, lost souls

My mind is broken
or maybe it's the heart I will blame on
this lapse of judgment that bears your name.
Take my hand and let's sin
without committing a sin.
We are free, restless
and the night is still young
even if we are old, lost souls.

Part III Body

That's a wicked pair of wings you have on you, baby.

Now take them off slowly and show me your sins.

No better place

There is no better place
to find myself
than under the roof
of your imperfections,
between the four walls
of your insecurities,
making love to you
on the floor of your doubts
until the only weakness you feel
is your trembling body under mine.

Under the cover

Everything starts and ends with words for her:

she appreciates waking up

to the smell of books in the morning…

and strokes herself to sleep

under their covers at night.

Misbehaving

That look she gives me–
the one meant for me to behave–
awakens my primal craving
that makes me want to
haul her over my shoulder
and drag her back to bed
to remind her
that I'm much better at misbehaving…

Silk & sin

When I look at you lying in this bed
wrapped in silk and sin
like a gift,
it's too easy for me to imagine
all those gods veiled by blue skies
never satisfied
with their offerings
save women's perfect form.

Shameless in love

I'm shameless in love:
my fingers will lead her boundaries
into temptation
and my teeth will nip at her limits
until they burn hotly
in the sweetest surrender.

Nothing ordinary

I see her wings

when she is undressing

before me,

but then I blink

and she is just an ordinary woman,

except

there is nothing ordinary about her.

Sharp edges

This world and I
are both made of sharp edges,
and I don't know about the world
but I am in search
of a tender-hearted woman
with soft hips
to cushion my hardness.

Challenge accepted

"You do know," I asked her,
"that telling me *no*
will sound a gong in my head,
flash a red sign in front of my eyes,
and the blood in my veins
will roar out its approval
in a challenge accepted?"
She smiled in answer.

Train wreck

She derailed my track of thoughts
with her cheeks turning pink.
I asked if she was blushing so prettily
everywhere.
Her answer left me a train wreck.

A dawn tastes like you

I have never been fond of mornings,
but then you stumbled out of my bed
and your lips covered mine.
Now, every time a morning greets me,
all I can think about
is that a dawn tastes like you.

Without words

Sometimes afterward
she wraps herself around me,
letting her hair fan out and drape
over my chest–
touching,
touching–
telling me without words
that I am hers.

Underneath my winter sheets

She burst on my tongue
like the perfect combination
of a sweet and tart blackberry
of late spring season
underneath my winter sheets.

Masks

Let's put on the masks, baby,

it matters not,

for I know your taste,

your scent.

Our bodies will always

recognize one another.

Not a civilized man

I am not a civilized man
when it comes to you, love,
an animal barely leashed.
I will whisper words of dark need
down your spine,
and bite your cheek hard enough
to make you blush
in remembrance
every time you sit on it.

Undone

She undid me

with the way she asked me

to touch her heart

softly

and her body

anything but that.

Plead for more

The only kind of begging
that should take place
in a relationship,
is when you are both spent
and breathless…
yet you plead for more.

Drumbeat

I want to singe your skin
with my touch,
burn the brand of my desire
into your very cells
until the wet heat of need between us
is a pulsing drumbeat
you can never again walk away from.

Madness beckons

She crosses her legs demurely
and the intimate susurration
of one silky thigh
rubbing against the other
sounds like an invitation.
Madness that beckons to sin,
and who am I to deny its call?

A rebel

I am a rebel, baby,
but I don't have a mad need
to burn everything to the ground.
The only fire
that makes the heart of arsonist in me
skip a beat
is this desire between you and me.
I want us to go up in flames.

Submission

She is a wild one
this woman of mine,
and taming her
has never even crossed my mind.
On occasion though,
I like to stroke her unruliness
into submission.

In the middle of the night

Even a restless soul like mine
needs an anchor;
a place I can call home,
a pair of arms
wrapped tightly around me
as if she never wants to let go,
those magnificent thighs
cradling me in the middle of the night.

Kiss & make up

We argue a lot,

kiss and make up even more,

for my hands

can't stay away from her

and her body

always gravitates toward me.

Distance is not a word

we've mastered in any language.

Deep waters

Watching her
wade into deep waters
fearlessly
spikes my desire.
All I want
is to be the very next wave
that will embrace her
and lap at her gently.

Demands

She gives me
everything I ask for,
and it might have spoiled me
senseless
had she not been making
her own demands in return.
Subtle, hotly feminine ones
a man has to pay careful attention
to pick up.
And it gives this man
an intense pleasure to heed them all.

A brand

A calm and silent night outside–
a storm raging from within
those four walls of the bedroom.
Her nails embedded in my flesh,
her teeth sunk into my skin,
as if every part of her
tried to anchor itself in me
and brand me
as much as I always brand her.

Red

Red might be the color
of sin to some,
but for me it's the shade of desire
that burns through my veins.
One look, one smile from her
is enough to ignite it
and run at full throttle.

The raw image of us

I want to fill your mind
with raw images of us;
limbs tangled,
mouths hungry.
I want to fill your soul
with yearning
as strong as the one I feel myself.
I want to fill your body…

My victory

It's all about those moments with her
that are worth waiting for.
I leave the daylight to bite the dust
and come to her with darkness
hiding the carnal beast
that awakens within me.
My hands turn into manacles
over her wrists,
leaving her deliciously helpless
and at my mercy.
Her body tells me wordlessly
that it's mine to command
and in my firm touch
lies the acceptance of her submission.

She is mine to please, to possess.
The world around us ceases to exist
and the only reality is pleasure
suffusing her expression,
in which I find my victory.

Drifting

Those long sleepless nights
have no beginning and no end in sight
to give us hope
and make us feel less like shipwrecks
on the cusp of loneliness.
Let me rock into you slowly.
We will drift toward the dawn together…

Out of the leash

I can't stop my lips from curving
when she throws a challenge at me
and gasps
finding herself with her wrists
imprisoned
behind her back.
Yet it's not my hold
that keeps her from struggling,
but her own need to let her arousal
slip out of its leash.

Limber flame

She is whispers
in the middle of the night,
sinful silk draped
across my feverish body.
She is limber flame
that sets us both on fire,
and I know not a greater pleasure
than the pain of this burn.

Anticipation

My needs run deeper, are a shade darker,
my touch is calloused and rough.
But her softness keeps me in check,
alleviating the voracious hunger
that always burns bright for her.
Yet tonight, she stays my hand
and the need reflected in her eyes
is my very own peering back at me
in its unapologetic glory.
Challenge is the language I speak fluently
and recognizing it in her every breath
makes my body go taut in anticipation.
I am an impatient man made of sharp edges,
filled with raw demands
and all that I am
is pushing me to take control.

But I push against the molten intimacy

of her touch instead

relinquishing the reins just this one time.

I let her do what we both desire…

Not much for subtle

I don't care much for subtle;
could never be satisfied with tasting life
one small bite at a time.
Hesitancy does not exist in my vocabulary–
I will absorb every nuance of my time here
and try to make the best of it.
I will devour you
until every inch of you
knows nothing… save my name.

Nothing but you

There are dark things in me
that ask for no permission
and the voracious hunger,
tearing me asunder,
wants to dine on nothing
but you.

Stroke for stroke

Perhaps I wished at times to hide those raw edges
under the veneer of civilization
and be the romantic kind of a lover
that women like to read about.
Perhaps. Maybe.
But I forget about all those women
when she looks at me
like I am the kerosene to her fire
and she wants no other
to ignite and assuage the inferno
that rages in her soul,
calling forth the savageness of my own.
Her softness is the answer to my maleness.
Stroke for stroke
we imprint our love on the world.

Red lipstick

The red lipstick of her smile
is a stop sign
that tells you to be cautious,
but dares you to come closer
and do it now,
because women like her
are not used to waiting.
Neither am I…

Wicked way

Some are afraid of passion,
claiming
that's the residing place of madness,
which once awakened,
consumes us–body, soul and mind.
If that's the case,
I say we stomp loudly to wake the beast
and let it have its wicked way with us.

Seduce her

Seduce her with your mind,

undress her with your words.

Render her speechless,

breathless,

yours…

before you set on touching her.

Bite marks

I am hers,

but it does not make me

any less of a wolf.

Sometimes the wild

can't be contained within

and she wakes up with bite marks

covering her flesh…

Too fierce love

Hers are the hours after midnight
when good girls
are meant to be asleep.
She belongs to wicked murmurs,
rough demands
and love too fierce to face the daylight.

Down to the last page

Her reading my mind
has certain advantages
and paints the most spectacular sight
to be held by me:
cheeks flushed,
breathing that escalates,
skin oversensitive, pulled taut over the body
that is my personal playground.
But it still pales in comparison
to the intoxicating way
she reads my soul–
down to the last page.

Poetry without words

Teeth,

fingers

grazing skin.

Lips,

bodies

pressed hard

against

one another.

Poetry made

without words.

Rated R

“I still believe in fairy tales,
why wouldn’t I?”
she looked at me with a little,
sinful smile.
“It’s just that now,
I prefer the kind
that has wicked words
spilling of its pages…”

White-hot trail

We love as ferociously as we fight:
handful of clothes–
gripping, ripping–
tongues dueling,
alternating the tempo
between slow and rough.
Domination is my middle name…
I can play and coax,
or I can demand a response from her
until she loses any thought
of ever holding back.
White-hot trail of need becomes us.

Dull conversations

"I'm tired of dull conversations
and mind-numbing, fleeting connection,"
she told me.
"Talk dirty to me,
stroke my mind into ecstasy,
so the echo of your words
will linger until next morning…"

Primal need

She is the temptation
living and throbbing under my skin.
The constant compulsion
I want to touch,
take and posses
until I know nothing
but this primal need
pulsating in my blood.

Uninhibited possession

She was not made for a lukewarm love:
she needs sensations
bursting through her like wildfire,
consuming not only her body,
but soul as well.
She wants her love now,
and she wants it hot enough
to leave scorched marks on the ground
where it hit after the two of you clash
in the fury of bold demands
and uninhibited possession.

This is how love is made

My fingers over her skin:

firm strokes,

lingering touches.

Worship without words,

beginning or the end.

This is how love is made.

A signature

She's awakened
a primal part in me,
the animalistic need
to mark my territory:
a dip of my head,
my lips finding their way to her neck–
kissing, suckling, teeth grazing
in such way that is surely to imprint
my signature on her…
and keep other predators at bay…

The world trembles

There is time for slow and easy,
but there is also time for taking an giving:
teeth sinking in,
breaths mingling,
bodies shuddering,
arms holding onto each other
while the world trembles and fades away…

The poem of her

My hands run over her body
trying to commit the shape,
the feel to my memory.
My fingers stroke her skin
failing at the attempt to write her
like the poem that she is.

Counting days and nights

Counting days and nights again…
those damn nights hold no rest for me
when I don't have your body
pinned underneath mine,
when your breath doesn't whisper
hot demands and sweet pleas over my skin.
I remember our last goodbye;
the way my lips claimed your mouth,
slid low, lower still…
my teeth finding this sensitive spot just below your ear,
sinking in concert with your gasp.
I wonder if the mark is still there?
It better be there when I am not…
Do you think of me
when I am not next to you?

Do you shiver at the memory
of my ghostly fingers
moving over the living silk of your skin?
Do you feel the pounding of my desire
or it's my longing, wistfulness–you name it–
doing all the talking?
It's a self-inflicted torture to think of you
when you are out of my reach.
It's a self-inflicted pleasure
that finds no relief.
It's far more than sex;
your absence is a gnawing ache in my gut.
I want you. I love you.
And right now I fucking hate you
for being so far away.

Slumbering beast

I like it:

all softness surrounding the spine of steel

that has fooled so many before me.

I love your scent of ice on a summer breeze

and exotic spice filling my mouth

on frigid nights when you let go

of the person the world thinks you to be

and awake the slumbering beast

that goes after what it wants.

Wolves mate for life

She loves feeling rays of sun
on her face,
but it doesn't make her heart race
like the sensation
of having moonlight on her bare skin
when we devour one another savagely
like those wolves that mate for life.

Open invitation

I am unable to take my eyes off
the way
your light moves seductively
in front of my dark:
lips curved in a knowing smile,
hips swaying in an open invitation
that even a saint would not deny,
and I am certainly not one.

Point of safety

Wake her up
with your voice in her ear
telling her things
that will make her blush
even in the middle of the dark.
Gild her skin with fire, with belonging,
for no matter the darkness,
your voice needs to be
the point of her safety.

Part IV Heart

To love me is to breathe the emotion into me,
so it would fill my hushed heart
with hope.

Beyond reason

There are women

that men have no choice

but to love beyond reason,

for they blow our minds away

with their scent,

taste,

sheer presence.

With arms wide open

I don't think I've ever known safe;
I recognize only edginess, respond to rawness.
I don't believe in feelings
until their ache is too much to bear.
Things don't feel real enough
unless I can touch, smell and taste them.
But I love the softness in you,
for I know there are demons
living under this tenderness of yours,
and they will welcome the unvarnished version of me
with arms wide open.

A mad girl

She was a mad girl
who would climb up the sky at night
to dance with the shimmering stars,
and kiss the moon goodnight
when the morning struck.
I was helpless
not to fall madly in love with her.

A woman well-loved

In my eyes
she is always desirable,
but she is never as glorious
as when her hair is messy
and she wears this secret smile
of a woman well-loved.

Don't let go...

Loving her body comes so easy.
Love her mind for all its complex thoughts.
Love her soul, her free spirit, the wild in her eyes
that hold your gaze with unasked questions like–
"can you handle all that I am?"
With an unspoken plea: "don't let go..."

Love is too pretty a word

Love is too pretty a word,
delicate like feelings easily hurt
and promises on the verge of fulfilling
or breaking.
The beast in me
is never satisfied with the pastels of it
until it can see the red
of your passion–
a little unhinged,
a whole lot honest.

She has my back

I look for them sometimes:
the chances lost,
the moments passed,
the people gone
and I wonder where did it all go.
Then I look at you and remember
those chances were more of misfortunes,
those moments dragged their feet
while I tried to move on
and those people have never had my back
the way you do.

Not your wolf

Darling,

I can not be your wolf,

for I have already found

my moon

and I howl for no other…

Every heartbeat

She always seems to worry
that the instant we are not together
the love we share goes to sleep
and my mind wanders off.
Baby, if you read this, know
that there is not a moment
I don't think about you
and my every heartbeat
bears your name.

I want to ruin her

What is love if not savaging another?
I don't want to be the first one she thinks about
when she opens her eyes in the morning.
Neither do I want to be the last on her mind
before she falls asleep.
I want to be the constant presence
walking even through her dreams,
while she remains unaware.
I want to be someone she can't breathe without,
can't recover from.
I want to ruin her for any other.
It seems only fair
since she has utterly and irreversibly
wrecked me.

A mating howl

You swear off love

and promise to never take

that wild ride again.

That's when the universe smiles,

stars start to whisper to each other

and the moon pulls a mating howl

from your throat…

Little signs

You are a half-finished cup of coffee
on the kitchen counter
with a smear of lipstick still over the rim.
A note left in a hurry
on the nightstand,
a scarf dropped carelessly
next to my tie.
You are a ribbon of your perfume
lingering in the air
that never quite fades away.
And my God,
there is nothing I love more
than those little signs
of your presence.

Center of the universe

My eyes

boring into hers

without blinking.

That's how a whole new universe

comes to life,

and she is the center of it.

Entangled

It's all entangled:
my hands–her hair,
the strings of my heart–her wrists,
and I wouldn't know
how to untangle it
even if I wanted to.

All feelings and no words

I can see love in her eyes
and it's a quiet kind
that comes out of its hiding place
sometimes
to perch on the tip of her tongue.
I try to catch it with my teeth,
but it slips away
every time.
Hers is the quiet kind of love–
all feelings and no words.

Drunk on love

Drunk on love;
I can't understand whether the earth spins
under my stumbling feet,
is it me revolving around it in madness,
or perhaps it's love itself.
Either way, I don't care–
pour me some more.

Wildly, recklessly, dangerously

Love me–

wildly,

recklessly,

dangerously,

on the verge of obsession–

as if the very thought of being without me

is causing your lungs to labor for breath

and your heart to stutter.

Then, and only then, you will know

how it feels to be loved by me.

Morning coffee

Her love tastes
like my morning coffee;
strong, with the first sip
that burns my tongue
and still makes me come back
for more.

Way home

Her heart is thunder in my ears;
louder still than my own,
and I wonder at times
how it is that someone
who has not been a part of us since our birth
can storm into our lives
and we welcome them with arms wide open
like a long–lost piece of ourselves
that has finally found its way home.

All or nothing

My love is a storm;
violent and all-consuming.
Once it starts,
all stop signs will fly away unheeded.
I don't do caution well–
I want all or nothing,
and it's something
that I will never compromise on.

The warmth of you

Restlessness is an old friend of mine
that aches to be comforted
by the old tricks like a drink or two.
But I reach for you instead,
and the whiskey has nothing
on the way your warmth
speeds through my veins.

This soft heart of hers

I love this soft heart of hers
that makes no assumptions
about words like *fine,*
but rather looks through her eyes
and makes its own judgment.
I'm worried about this soft heart of hers
that always tries so hard to understand
and justify the world around her
while the world around her
too often simply doesn't give a fuck.

True north

My feet will always bring me back
to you,
for my body carries a compass
in the shape of a human heart,
and you are my true north.

Spectacular flight

We were a tragedy waiting to happen,
a train about to wreck,
one midair step away from the edge.
But when we fell…
Ah, baby, when we fell,
it was the most spectacular flight
two human beings can take.

An exhibitionist

Some say that love is crazy
and they are better off without it
while they long for it in private.
I say it's mad, downright insane,
but the need for your brand of loving
is too strong to ever pine for it secretly.
I am an exhibitionist
when it comes to you, love,
and I don't care who knows it.

Previous life or another

The echo of your footsteps
is so familiar,
we must have started the journey
toward each other
in one previous life or another…

Nothing of safety

She is safe within the walls of my heart
focused on tender loving.
It's my mind she should be wary of,
for it's filled with dark, dangerous thoughts
of consuming her,
and it knows nothing of safety.

Seeing stars

"How could I not

believe in magic,"

she told me,

"when the way, in which our bodies

are pressed together,

makes me see the stars…"

Midnight muse

She is my midnight muse;
the lover I always turn to
with need in my eyes,
fever guiding my hands
and greedy mouth
that spills poetry onto her skin…

The way you hold her

It's the way you hold her:
like one might a breath,
with reverence,
an utter possession.
Don't hide your intentions
whatever they might be.
She will deal with your eagerness better
than translating your hesitation
into the beginning of the end…

Moonstruck

She speaks stars and I can see
constellations in the depth of her eyes.
She is a daughter of the universe
that leaves me moonstruck.

Unless you mean it

Don't offer me your love
unless you mean it.
People fall because going down is easy,
but love is a steep climb
and if you slip up
you need to start all over again.
I'm not for quitters,
not for faint-hearted either.
Sometimes, I am not even for myself.
Be sure, be very sure
before you offer me your love
unless you mean it.

Collide into me

There is more than enough space
in this universe,
but I do hope you will collide into me.
I want to taste the stars on your lips
and fall into the midnight of your eyes.
Collide into me,
I can hardly wait
for this shattering experience.

Put your money where your mouth is

I have so much to say to you
that sometimes I will go quiet,
not because I can't find the right words,
but because I think you deserve more than words alone.
You deserve someone who will stay at your side
even when everyone else is gone–
especially then because, baby,
screw what they think.
You don't need to prove yourself to anyone,
it's all about living your truth the way you choose to,
and not letting others dictate who you are
until you no longer know it yourself.

You deserve someone
who will walk you through the hardest times of your life
instead of only waiting for you unscathed
on the other end of it.
You deserve someone who you can trust to be there
the next morning when you wake up,
even if he was not there to tuck you in
the night before.
You deserve someone…
and I am not saying that I deserve you,
but you know that I'm not the walking away type
and it's not my ego talking,
but determination born out of love I have for you.
I just want to spend the rest of my life
on putting my money where my mouth is.
Let me?

A hunger like no other

With her, a night is never just a night anymore:
it's an adventure,
without beginning or the end in sight.
It's longing while being together,
and there is no such thing as apart.
She awoke a hunger like no other
in the lone wolf within me,
oblivious to everything
but love and the next full moon
that never wanes.

The edge of forever

The look in her eyes
makes me think of words
I want to put into sentences,
turn into lyrics,
for she is the music
I want to dance to
until the edge of forever.

Love her right

Love her with the intensity of stars
that burn, but never fall.
Love her with the madness of words unsaid,
yet expressed and exchanged in raw kisses
that leave lips bruised with the sweetest kind of ache.
Love her with violence that will always feel tender
on her sensitive skin.
Love her well and love her right.

Pull of her moon

She seduced me

into the brink of forever:

I was just water

before she turned me into the tide

that can't resist the pull of her moon.

Imperceptible

I don't want our love
to be something explainable or tangible,
so that others would feel tempted
to lay their dirty hands on it and taint it
with things, memories, people and places
that have nothing to do with you or me.
I am perfectly fine with it
being this something imperceptible
that it is transferred in looks across the room
and secret smiles nobody can understand but us.

Wolves underneath

We are wolves underneath this skin, my love,
wearing darkness close to our bones,
wrapping moonlight around our hearts
and pulling love songs out of the throats
that might go hoarse with longing at times,
but will never go silent.

Prove them wrong

Loving someone
doesn't mean pretending
they are perfect and have no flaws,
but kissing those parts
they deem unworthy
to prove them wrong...

The luckiest bastard

I always say she belongs to me,
but the truth is that a woman like her
does not belong to anyone or anything
but herself.
Her mind, soul and heart are always shifting,
roaming free,
even when she seems firmly anchored in reality.
Life can hold her back on occasion,
but in the end, she always goes where she wants to,
does what she was meant to do.
And the fact she chooses to come back to me
day after day,
makes me the luckiest bastard in every universe.

When she comes undone

Love her until all of her pieces–
that threaten to fall apart–
feel secure in the knowledge
there are hands waiting to catch them
and put back together
when she comes undone.

Sirens blaring in warning

Our love has never been a gentle breeze
or softness of the rain.
We are thunderstorms,
lightning slashing the sky
and sirens blaring in warning.

The fabric of forever

Our souls
carry the imprint of one another:
mine is stained by the red of your love,
yours is drenched in the black ink I use
to write us into the fabric of forever.

Unapologetically

The chaos in her soul

might be a subtle thing,

but it doesn't lessen her need

to be loved wildly,

recklessly

and unapologetically.

The trembling bones of your rib cage

And if he wants to explore you–let him,
but remember
that the expanse of your skin
is not meant to be traveled in one day,
and that the trembling bones
of your rib cage
need even more care and time
to part and reveal the vulnerability
of your heart.

A field day

Love her,

especially in those places

she calls ugly,

in the corners of her mind

where all her insecurities

have a field day.

Every. Single. Day.

Fighter of a lost cause

One of the things I love about her the most
is that she is a fighter of a lost cause:
she roots for an underdog,
walks hand in hand with a rebel
while we are seeking Wonderland
where we could all just be
whatever and whoever the hell we want to,
without the world demanding we fit in.

The aching places

You deserve a lover

who will not pretend

the past did not happen,

but rather take care

while touching the aching places

it has left behind.

I want it all

I can't just love you–

I'm too obsessive and possessive for that.

Love trembles and pales in your presence,

can't look you in the eye.

But this is not me.

You know I will dare you

to take your eyes off me

while I devour you one small bite at a time,

so that those parts of you

nobody has ever braved to explore,

will understand that when I say

I want it all–

I mean it.

Enough for two

I don't expect logic

from this heart of mine:

it has faltered too many times to count,

or to be taken seriously.

But it can love,

ah, can it love.

Yet even in this,

it seems to be beating only for one,

and still make it enough for two.

When it rains too hard

"I don't know what to do
about the vulnerability of my heart,"
she tells me,
looking as sad as I've ever seen her.
I guess that's what happens to people
when they gamble on the fragility
of their own bones and learn how much pain
the breaking really brings and how long it lasts.
I had a broken heart, nursed broken bones too
and they all ache in a sensory memory
when it rains too hard.
We all want the glory of love
but wish the hurt–that catches the same train
and travels as a stowaway–
will plague someone else.

Until the bitter end

This love of mine
might feel too intense at times:
it walks the thin line
of obsession on some days,
drives at full tilt
the highway of devotion always.
What it has never been is a manipulating tool,
a guilt trip, an abductor to hold you hostage.
If you want to leave,
I will fight to the bitter end,
but I would never want to keep someone,
at all costs,
who doesn't want to stay.

Messy morning

I fell in love with her
on a messy morning
when she was running late
with this wild look in her eyes
that told me she was in a dozen different places
at the moment,
yet she still lingered long enough
to kiss me goodbye.

Tsunami waves

Maybe my heart was quiet and steady
like those hands
but it's all in the past;
now they tremble in unison
every time you give me that look
that promises earthquakes
to rock my world
and tsunami waves
to crash at my shore.

Too tame a word

Love is too tame a word,
lust seems like an itch to scratch,
and what you are
is a temptation to touch,
a compulsion to taste
over and over.
A constant beat in my blood.

Skinny dipping

The stars
move in waves tonight–
the sky parts their blueness for them.
And all I want
is to climb up there
and skinny-dip with you.

Pick-me-up

She would steal love words
away from the poems that I wrote for her,
whenever she thought me unaware
(I always was).
She would then secretly press them
between the pages of her favorite books
like dried flowers
and use as a pick-me-up on those days
she needed more tenderness than usual.

Mine

I've been called many a name
by people who barely knew my real one
and I've never cared much for any of them.
But the way she calls me *hers*
struck such yearning in me
that it has finally awoken
this greedy beast of my heart.
Its sluggish rhythm staggers to right itself
and beat back:
mine
mine
mine...

You got yourself a warrior

You got yourself a warrior, baby.
Now you will know
what it's like to be loved
without mercy,
with a hint of ruthlessness,
a bite of savage
and a whole lot of feral protectiveness.

There are days

There are days
when she is more prickly thorns
than a rose.
It's when I hold her tighter,
love her more fiercely…
while I wipe her tears away
with my bloodied fingers.

Bloodstream

I'm unsure how,

but the ink

that was meant to write you out

of my veins,

only managed to burrow you deeper

into my bloodstream.

The temple of her heart

I will love her
underneath her skin,
in the sanctuary of her veins,
in the cradle of her ribs
until I reach the temple of her heart
and lay my own in offering.

88870376R00164

Made in the USA
Columbia, SC
05 February 2018